JOHN FIGUEROA

THE CHASE

a

Collection of Poems
1941 - 1989

Part I: The Chase

Part II: Utopia

Part III: Ars Longa

Part IV: Vita Brevis

A M D G
ad maiorem Dei gloriam

and for
Alexander Murry — Dorothy Grace

PEEPAL TREE

First published in 1992
Peepal Tree Press
17, King's Avenue
Leeds LS6 1QS
Yorkshire
England

ISBN 0 948833 52 1

ACKNOWLEDGEMENTS

Many of these poems have been published before in Anthologies, in Journals and in the author's books, *Love Leaps Here*, and *Ignoring Hurts*. The Journals in question include: *Ambit, America, BIM, Caribbean Quarterly, The Caribbean Writer, Cross Currents, Focus, The Holy Cross Purple, Kyk-over-Al, London Magazine, Revista Interamericana*. Some poems have also been broadcast on the B.B.C. Many thanks to all who have helped getting these poems into print or on the air.

Nec satis apparet cur versus factitet, utrum
Minxerit in patrios cineres, an triste bidental moverit
incestus.

I: THE CHASE

II: UTOPIA

III: "ARS LONGA"

IV: "VITA BREVIS"

I: THE CHASE

THE CHASE

Confusing love, by love confused
Refusing love, by love refused
Pursuing love, by Love pursued.

No mystic I
Not for lack of wanting, but
I find the body's thrust
Through woods of light and shade enchanting,
        Confusing love, by love confused.

No mystic I
Not for lack of trying, but
Compulsive I prove
My flimsy truths — and others' lying,
        Refusing love, by love refused.

No mystic I
But after wine, flesh and dancing
Post coital sadness singing
I know how chance and meaning mesh,
        Pursuing love, by Love pursued.

January 1977

STONE HILLS, ON NEARING JOS, NIGERIA

Breast-like hills, hard
Rounding from flatness, awaken
Dry and sleepy travellers

Suddenly, amidst green plains
(Matrix of upright sticks
Tasselled with dun, and brown)

Back-breaking wanderings
Home to excitement, rest
(Quiet breathing after)

Rosebuds taut and flushed

Arousing love
With love aroused

SPRING FEAST

When the Roman soldier laughed
And showed his money
I was Magdalene.

When Judas counted coins
With double-entry envy,
Finding no means to appropriate,
I was he.

I was Peter
When he warmed himself
By the burning coals
And looked not at the accusing maid.

I was the darkened sun,
My heart the riven earth.
Now I am the Easter sun arisen
The wind-tipped eagle
Scalloping across the sky.

Magdalene I was,
Judas, Peter;
Now I am the risen Lord.

INSIGHT

To see you naked is to sight
an island of essential things
and have the grace of wings
to float and soar across
the currents where the careless die.

Waves of light waves of sea
break, break eventually
upon your unveiled body
balanced between dream and blinding light.

The mind of man
must catch the light
to know the constant aspiration of
the running seas for still mountains
the bright urges across mangrove swamps
towards the scrubby plains
that slightly rise
and rising point
to dread divinities

rigid in their veils.

To see you is to know
how base swamps and fresh waters grow
towards each other, how the flow
from choppy shallows across deeps,
of some thing born of water and of air,
pulls us to the peaks.

Waves of light waves of sea
break, break eventually
upon your unveiled body
balanced between dream and blinding light.

To see you is to sight
a land of shadowy keeps,
and have the grace of wings
to float and soar across
the narrows where the careless die

and flutter gently down,

travel-dry,

surprised at last,

by peaks unveiled,

the sap-like ease

and subtle springs.

CHRISTMAS BREEZE

Auntie would say "Ah! Christmas breeze",
as the Norther leapt from the continent
across Caribbean seas,
across our hills
to herald Christmas,
ham boiling in the yard
plum pudding in the cloth
(Let three stones bear the pot;
and feed the hat-fanned fire).

This breeze in August cools a Summer's day
here in England.
In December in Jamaica
we would have called it *cold*,
Cold Christmas Breeze,
fringing the hill tops with its tumble
of cloud, bringing in
imported apples, and dances
and rum (for older folk).
For us, some needed clothes, and a pair
of shoes squeezing every toe.
And Midnight Mass:
Adeste Fideles!

Some Faithful came —
and why not? — a little drunk,
some overdressed, but
ever faithful.
Like Christmas breeze
returning every year, bearing
not August's end, nor October's
wind and rain but, Christmas
and 'starlights'

and a certain sadness, except for Midnight Mass
and the Faithful
('The Night when Christ was born')

I miss celebrations, but I miss most
the people of faith
who greeted warmly every year
the Christmas breeze.

August 1982

CLARITY

Now leaves have fallen I can see
the architecture of trees,
how dark earth pumps sap slowly to
the sun and skies.

    The tracery of
black branches, tiny, relieved
with berries red & brown on the pulse
of stripping winds, dyes my window
to cathedral dreams.

    (After cleansing winter, the literature of leaves,
    and all that deafening shimmer of silk!)

I prefer you stripped like winter,
stripped to what the heart's pump
pushes through bone and flesh
from pirouet to pirouet,
from stoop to tall standing,
silence to inward speech.

BERRIES OLD OR NEW?

My tree has lost the white
of blossoms, petals torn
away and strewn across
the garden walk.

Revealing winds, that turn
green leaves over, expose
hard knots, green and white,
that promise fruit,
        and hanging
there, concealed in calmer times,
red wrinkled berries.

        Are survivors
an old or new generation?

When wind turns undersides
of leaves, what do you see,
in morning's silver shine?

        Lasting fruit,
or promises of white dreams?

INVADERS

The fall of snow we cannot hear
the flow of fear we cannot see

surround and mystify the sere
marrow of ancient bones that creak.

And through the stretching flesh
the searching waves, uncertain, seek

the contours of a willing beach
to welcome and protect a mesh

of whisperings and rounding ways.

Beyond the trees in a shaded creek
a warm blush lights a prow,

and crystal waves —
the storms as yet undreamed —
caress a brazen bare canoe

silent as snow
                    insidious and new.

HARTLANDS/HEARTLANDS

The flash of sound across
The city streets, the train
Shunting miles away —

Shoulder against the warm wall
I dreamt of trains that crossed
Our little country:
            Bushy Park
            Grange Lane
            Hartlands
                Spanish Town
                Olden Harbour
            May Pen
            Four Paths
                Kendal ....

After that, the summer stop
For Spauldings,
The stations are not so
Easily recalled
But certainly there
Were also
            Frankfield
            Siloh
                Mount Pellier
                  Cambridge
                    Mo Bay

The screech the flash
The whistle would wake me

Then I'd recall the Summers
at Mrs Caine's oblivious of the others
In the heat and confusion of Kingston.

Now and again in strange cities
The sudden release of steam
The rush of the horn
Recalls it all

Bushy Park
Grange Lane
Hartlands
        Heartlands
        Heartlands

Spanish Town
Port o' Spain
Port au Prince
Point à Pitre

        Grange Lane
        Bushy Park
Hartlands
        Heartlands
                Heartlands

King's Cross St Pancras
Gare St. Lazare
Gare du Nord
Gare de Lyons
        Zaragoza
        Port Bou
        Port Bou
                Narbonne

Gare Mont Parnasse
        Dieppe/Newhaven
        Dieppe/Newhaven

                    Dieppe/Newhaven
Victoria Victoria Victoria
King's Cross St Pancras
Gare St. Lazare
Gare du Nord
Gare de Lyons
            Zaragoza
            Port Bou
            Port Bou
                    Narbonne

Gare Mont Parnasse
                    Dieppe/Newhaven
                    Dieppe/Newhaven
                    Dieppe/Newhaven
Victoria Victoria Victoria

                    Bushy Park
                        Grange Lane
                            Hartlands
                                Spanish Town
                                    Olden Harbour
                                    Olden Harbour
                                        Hartlands

Heartlands Heartlands
                        Heartlands

ROOTS AND MOVEMENT

In shaded woods my friend
digs. Seeks his roots.

After much sweat following
tortuous dark tubes
fork-tongued like snakes
he finds.

Anchored he smiles at the frisky lion,
watches the lively birds dart,
and eagles like mercury
slowly rolling back and forth
across the inverted bowl of sky.

He's rooted, unmoved
awaits high winds,
and warm ministrations of dogs
planting their territorial flags.

Ah! rockaby baby
in the tree top
when the wind blows the cradle will
rock the well-rooted to sleep,

dreaming of ancestral chiefs,
while lions roar and pounce
and horses tamed by Hector
arch over walls,

and metal birds freely streak
far over rooted trees
like lions leaping across
the turbulence of streams.

NON STAR

When heroine and hero come
on stage the playwright sends
me packing. I get lost

I am the frost on the cake
not the icing. I entice

in early action, drop a name
or two to set important people
talking. The critics find

my mind and character
underdeveloped. Perhaps a trace

of elements no longer
active — unapparelled,
en passage, when rich and weary take
their comfort and their bows.

I shall no doubt be called
to hold a curtain as

applause puffs up
well paid parties.

What, darling, would we do
without the minor parts
and lesser talents?

Deconstruct, I suppose, the play,
or reconstruct the monetary balance.

(May/June 1987)

THE LADIES OF SPAIN

At the table sipping
In Chicote in Madrid
The women are waiting
(Not dreaming of anything like sex
Despite the revealed ravines
Running through the rolling
Country of their breasts!)
They wait pulling skirts over
Crossed and recrossed knees.
They try; dust dry privately
And in their hearts.

Are there harder ways to paradise?

Today at Avila, where St. Theresa
Made no bones about her beauty,
I nearly violated the cloister
Helping two workmen with their barrow
I found myself at the open door
Mother Superior waving me away

Locked within leaning forward
Waiting facing us two still
Vases each a nun
Completely veiled in black

At first I thought them dummies
But they waited, held themselves,
Still as quiet vases,
Persistent as St. Theresa,
Beyond movement or rest.
Are there easier ways than Carmelite
Of winning heaven?

God, who made us all,
Those who are whores and nuns
And those who walk between fearing both
Not knowing how to wait not knowing
How to give all, obliterate self,

Out of the clear distinct drought
Of high León and the confusion
Of cities and the wet heat
Of coastal countries edging tropic seas

Bring us together in your love
All who serve or think they serve
In such strange ways.

BIRTH IS...

Birth is too bloody; we resist the end
The throes, the after-birth and after-care
Of child and mother. Darkly unaware
We start the perfumed path whose sudden bend
At dawn to us reveals the unknown friend.
The agony of mother and child we fear,
We are solicitous, nor God nor air
We trust: without security we will not lend

Our precious selves to poor posterity.
Suppose our seed to Faith should swell
And make demands on our temerity!

Or throes like waves should dash the spell
That dreams ourselves the final verity
Against infinite shores to splintered shell.

London, 1950

THE DANCE

The smell of powder
And parfum
The firm gentle pressure of your breasts
But more the release
In the steady leaning on the pattern
Of the music
To become free
Of the music's pattern.
We whirl through the spaces
Between planet and planet
Our opposition
Our opposite pressures
Different sides of the wave
Sloping upward to the crest
That does not break
While the music lasts
Our thesis and antithesis
By opposing end themselves
Resolve themselves in the dance
We, more than our single movements,
Have built from our parallel forces
Not a parallelogram
But a perfect, endless circle.

WHERE VENUS CASTS HER THICKETS TO THE SEAS

The mount of Venus shapes us all
One rests there as on swaying seas
Asleep awake one dreams of wooded slopes
Or thickets buzzing with the bees.

The bareness of the slope at times
The inscooped corner of a col
The columns and breezes of these climbs
Are living with her dreams and his

And so the movement grows and groans
And tips across the broken heights
Above clear lakes and sparkling stones.

The mountains are not male
The shaded thickets are not hers,
A cup of wine is not enough
The broken image, floating, stirs
Rising to seek its other self.

And though each half of God-divided wholes
Will tell you how autonomous it breathes
Together they will find their restless souls
Where Venus casts her thickets to the seas.

Mexico/El Centro 1974

PSALM 120: A SONG FOR PILGRIMS

I look at their mountains;
Where shall I find my help?
My help is in the Lord
The Lord who makes mountains,
And seas, planets and stars

The Lord keep you from stumbling
The Lord of Israel
Who never sleeps.

Fear not the noon-day sun
Nor the disturbing moon,
For his shadow falls between

May he shade and guard you now;
Your coming and going, now,
And evermore
Amen

WRITTEN AT SEA

For Jack Berry
and in Memoriam the Russian Cosmonauts

Exegi monumentum...
Horace, III, 30. *Carmina.*

Grant you must my claim
Proud but perfectly achieved,
It is not Lignum Vitae that I seek
But living laurel to cover
my lost hair.

All of me will not die
More than remains survive
My funeral rites. This quiet
Fame will grow while the Pontiff
Measures in meditation
The steep mountain
And the virgin church is full
of silence.

O they will speak of me
As the man who heard
Across the harsh shushing
Of the seas from this dry land—
Dryly ruled—the broken line
Of Horace and his consonants
Clustering with maturing promise

For he, a colonial, also colonised
An imperial tongue
And led distant rhythms
To breed upon his own.

O dear Jack I have built
A monument more lasting than bronze
Standing taller than the royal
Resting place of the Pharaohs,

Your dripping rain
And the strong sirocco, impotent,
Cannot wear it out nor
All the *saecula saeculorums*

Nor time itself like a flying-fish
Skimming so many, but too few,
Of the spray-twisted out-stretched crests
Of this oncoming cobalt sea.

"PASTORES"
(After St. John of the Cross)

For Hunter Francois

Shepherds on the green
Have you my lover seen?
If you meet him on the slopes
Freeing sheep from stony cotes
Tell him I cannot reach the heights
I am hungry, I am weak, the flights
Of birds no longer cheer me.
For I do not have him near me.

Hasten down the hillside
Lover mine to the millside,

Where I, hungry, see my face
In the stream that has the grace
To fool me not, to show me that
Without you I am not.

"EL PECHO DEL AMOR MUY LASTIMADO"
(after St. John of the Cross)

He weeps not for an ancient love
His grief is present, heart
Could not be desiccated so
For old days and
His heart so parched for love.

He remembers that he is
Forgotten by her loveliness:
His brown complaint, his present drought
And his heart so parched for love.

She forgets, flourishing in green mirages;
No hope for this desert land
But to climb the rigid tree
And water with his blood
His heart so parched for love.

PORTRAIT OF A WOMAN (AND A MAN)

Firmly, sweetly
refusing...
Tall for seventeen fit
for a tumble

"A guess hard time
tek her" she said
referring to
her mother's misfortune
(Her strict mother whose
three men had left
her holding five
pledges to fortune.)

She came easily into
my arms
refusing only to kiss

"Any familiarity an
we stop right now"

Dixerat— as lacrymae rerum used to say.
She's in the public domain
She's lost her patent rights
but would not kiss

"A guess hard time tek her"

Love, yes
Tenderness, no.
Mating's fine
Involvement, woe.
Familiarity would spoil
The moment's glow.

"A guess hard time tek her"

She is in the public domain
She's copied, copied, copied.

"You have bad min'
Doan tell nobody
Doan tell nobody
Doan mek mi do it
    mek mi
Doan mek mi do it
    mek mi
lawd:

You see I intend to be
a nurse
No need to apologise
(Lawd it sweet!)

But if you try to kiss
me I will scream."

OUR MOTHER IS THE HEAVENLY JERUSALEM A CITY OF FREEDOM

It is written that Abraham had two sons, one by a slave and the other by a free woman. But while the son of the slave was born according to the flesh, the son of the free woman was born because of the promise: this is an allegory.

Paul, *Galatians 4:22,23.*

Logic is the mind's
honesty
(after the white
sowing of seed)
the birth of thought
by promise
commitment to
consequences:
the branching of the blood
the building of the brain
after care and
after birth of
child and mother

"Will you love me?
will you care for
what this coming
together must bring—
the bruising of the flesh
the losing of our cool
of ourselves—
the openness
the openness
to earth
to death
to birth

(when you have divided me
disturbed the turbulent
ocean from whose green
boiling the firm
and gentle shape
diaphanous as dawn
clean as first light
lifts at the stroke
of the wand
the wand that hurts and heals)
are you willing
to wait to hold
to nurse secrets
and secret power
that you and I
alone have shared?

Will our minds
follow freely
committed
to consequences
(after the white
sowing of seed)
the crystals whose
shapes we do not
choose except in
choosing crystals
(the mocking bird
awakes the green
exactness of
the guango tree—
I choose to listen—
but the guango
        does not grow from

an almond seed
and I choose not
to follow the noise
of a passing bus)

Logic is the mind's
honesty

The son of the free
Is born in promise
The parent slave
Inconsequentially

Tortola/Mona 1968

"I HAVE A DREAM"
COLUMBUS LOST
OR
ALL O' WI A SEARCH

The Afrocentric finds great pleasure in
(And laughs assuring self and clientele)
Reminding us that Colon had lost
His way
So stupid was Columbus, lost
European, he called these nightingale
Places the Indies (West)
(Later others finding snakes
In Haiti thought their kindly Gods
Had crossed the seas
Weaving worship of the phallic kind
From Africa.

The Minoan Goddess, gold
And light, loved serpents too!)
The man so fool yu si
Him tink a India him come!
And touring Europeans of the wandering kind
(Some are black and some are white)
Find Africa, neither East nor West,
Just Africa, in these seas.

But him so fool yu si
Him tink a India him come.

How easy to travel far
And not arrive at where you are
(Some nowhere finding home)
To escape and not achieve our goal
Is intolerable: India or Africa.

To search is, or is not
To find.

But to build up
Ourselves by showing
How foolish others are...
(The man so fool yu si
Him tink a India him come)

The certainties that seem so firm
The Afro-cut, Dashiki and the like,
Eroded by constant winds
That blew before Colon and before you,
Will slush away to sea
In sudden gullies with the steeps
You have not terraced,
With the blessed water from your hills
Soiled, unhusbanded.
Colon, ventured by caravel
You read, tossed by wind rushes from
Disturbed persons talking.

The whole heap o' wi
So fool you si, mi chile,
We tink a India wi come
Or Africa
An' all the while
A home wi deh, a home
Yu neber lose yet, nu?

Mek sure a weh you deh
As the man say
Are you ashamed because you're lost

(Laughing at others!) Can you
Forget the fading of the dream
Forget the wavering of the quest
Deep into the unknown
Through tangled forests and empty seas
Amidst amazing currents where
The pointing of the path,
The firmness of the feet, depend
On bursts of bird-song shifting shifting...

St. Thomas/Cidra/Mona (March-May 1972)

FROM THE CARIBBEAN WITH LOVE

The carrion crow
        the john crow
Is caught up above
        the tree tops
By rushing rollers'
        breaking
Invisible foam
        and blown spume
Of turbulent air
        like ocean's
Unsteady ascents
        and tumblings
With pinions asserting
        selfhood
And levelling the surge
        of Sea/Air
The balancing bird
        achieves glide
Is master of air
        and ocean
In circling the blue
        the john crow
Controls all the waves
        and big winds
Disturbed alone
        by dead flesh

In circling the blue
        the john crow
Controls all the waves
        and big winds
Disturbed alone
        by dead flesh

In circling the blue
        the john crow

The velvet delay
        of hovering
The thrust of the tip
        on wide sweep
Wing out-stretched
        to upmost
And climbing the wave
        the john crow
So gently so calm
        on wave top
Disturbed alone
        by dead flesh
Is motionless save
        for small head
So knowing and peeled

The carrion crow—
        the john crow
With one foot atop
        the carcass
the beak so acute
        in searching
the entrails that have
        no secrets
the tiny so red
        so shrivelled
And knowing, so old,
        the john crow's
Efficient head
        draws out
At length implications

rarely
Exposed involutions
pale guts.

In circling the blue
the john crow
Controls all the waves
and big winds
Disturbed alone
by dead flesh
In circling the blue
the john crow

The velvet delay
of hovering
Unbalanced disturbed
by dead flesh
The movement now so tiny
so hurried
Atop the unburied offal.

Yet all flesh must turn
to maggots
And john crows so soon
return to
A mastering of air and ocean.

Every jon crow t'ink 'im pickny white
Every spree boy
say fi him rungles right
Every 'homan who ketch
him bes' fren' man
So positive 'im mumma
An' all de worl' will understan'

How close to the carrion
blue skies
hesitation to glide

We are part and parcel
of searching
For what keeps us going and dying

The seducer's voice is smoother
Than circling of crow
the dead flesh
Of teaser reveals less
than carrion.

The delicately balanced ships
Circle the green seas
before the perfumed breezes
Rigging stretched and creaking
in the longed-for trades
Sliding circling
till the smell of loot
Shortens the sail
and the islands become carrion
Plucked at, investigated
searched
The entrails greedily beaked
for gold
The ships are glorious in
their circling
(As the slavers must have seemed
to the unknowing
As they rounded it to Elmina)
But they are squat

unbalanced
Atop the prize
the offal

We have sprung from the urge
To know the entrails
We are proud of such ancestral
errors
As bred us here . . . .
Proud? Why be proud
of what
You or I could not
did not
And would have done?
We must know
While not denying the nurture
Of history and the permanent peace
Of a lawn cared for for a thousand years
We must know the span of now
As many depend on the stretch
Backward nearly forever.

We know many peoples, many tribes
We are them. We are witnesses to
The new annointment that came
With Christ:
The love
From doubtful births,
From the human desire
To put away the strange
Paternity,
From the infinite
Receptivity of woman

Who knows more than can be known
We witness that no human mixture
Is miscegenation
That what comes out of a man
                defiles:
Alien for brothers;
Mine for ours
Race for culture.

We know and must remember
That within us
The enemy lurks
We know that we are no
Better and no worse

We know the john crow does
His work
But that is not our lot

We seek no enemy abroad
But as all must
Watch the enemy within
The certainty of ignorance
The large claims of smallness
The desire to be master

Or slave
The temptation to forget
Too little
Or to remember too much
To imitate those we
Say we do not honour
So as to prove

what needs no proving
That we are God's children
as free and as bound
As all our brothers.

There are three things
I do not understand
The way of crows in the air
The way of ships in the sea
The way of man
With man
Aye and there is a fourth
that I should claim
Not to understand.

How close to carrion
blue skies
hesitation to glide
We are part and parcel

Breadfruit from the South Seas
Mangoes from the East
Salt fish from Canada
Afu from Africa
Rice from Spain
Curry from India

Through searching, that gave us birth,
Let us know our meaning
and love it
(It is the world's)

Let us put on the new man

(When the breadfruit season come
you know say hungry done)

Jack Mandora

a dis one

mi a choose!

LOVE LEAPS HERE . . .

The white rain leapt over the hills
Over the blue and green hills
And settled on my house.

The sky had been clear and pale
No clouds or mist gave distance to
Distant hills whose stubble backs
I could have stroked, it seemed,
By stretching anticipating hands
Through the show-windows of my house.

The white rain leapt over the hills

So suddenly, too, from paleness
And nearness of distant breasts of Earth
Eros leaps settling on
My house.

Silent at first the white rain
And then insistent, sharp.

For Greeks, and for me, at times
Aphrodite has leapt out of foaming sea

But now over the hills
Suddenly leaping over hills
Like cloudless white showers
Silent at first, drumming after
Love seizes and batters;
It is from dry earth
Touched with the white shower
That Venus surges up
Possessing the land like Spring.

Love leaps here suddenly and
Like the unexpected shower,
Rages and nourishes
Leaving the sky so pale
The hills so green and blue.

THE TRIPLE BIRCH
OR
EPIPHANY

I

Trinity white, who framed you thus?
Who set the centre-line, the focus point,
Who daubed your wood-paint, struck your green flame,
Against this never quiet wood,
Upon the milk-full breasts of earth,
Below heaven's blazing orchard?

II

Tasting the salt sweat of my brow,
As stretched for a moments's rest grabbed from pots
        and pans,
Or rolling from a frenzied dream of a mind tired of pots
        and pans,

Oh triple birch,
Framed by my window,
I saw you glisten white.
Whether rising up on elbow
At dawn I saw you,
Oh triple candle-stick,
Burning white before the swaying green
And black of forest and its shadows;
Or, sleepless, saw your fingers coil
About heaven's diamond sands,
Sometimes letting them slip to glow and glide,
Pebbles tossed into a phosphorescent sea.
I saw you shine at dawn
And you were more than falling stars:
In my cathedral burning, blazing white,
Not beehive formed, nor moulded whale fat,

But from the snows' whiteness robbed
And stored away in roots,—
The Master dead, and Pontius Pilate king,
(Oh I am tired of pots and pans,

Of fingers shrivelled in soap suds burning,
Of pots burnt-food-crusted)
His washed fingers calming
A dream worried wife—

In my cathedral blazing bright
You shone
Alone in the early gloom,
Beneath the black clouds bulging,
Among the gaping tombs and their wayless wandering
    fruit,
You shone morn and night;
More comforting than all the human hands.

III

You shone a night and I turned
And nodded and went to dream
Of jasmine fields where supple backs never burn,
Of peaceful lily shores washed by the white of the sea.
At dawn, the battering, beating of a hammer and
The squench of nails,
And in my window frame
No birch bark gleamed,
No leaves shivered, green tongues
Of flame wavering on the white torch tree,
For the triple birch was gone
Carpenter-cut, neatly, corded for the fire.

IV

But still shine on, oh triple candle-stick.
The bones have been numbered,
And none broken; Joseph has lent his tomb...
"Destroy this temple and in three days..."
Raise up they triple prong
In the blackness of this holy night
In this easter eve cathedral,
Let three stars be thy flame,

And every blowing breeze, blooming bud,
Bursting star sing out
        Lumen Christi,
        Lumen Christi,
        Lumen Christi,
For when sweat was brine for choking breath
When sleep was swamp of slime,
Swamp of thoughts seed-barren in sun
But bunch-clustered at night,
A triple birch tree shone,
A trinity white,
At dawn more than the singing of birds
At night than falling stars.

BLUE MOUNTAIN PEAK REVISITED, 1943

I

Everlasting hills who desire only Him,
Everlasting hills here stubborn before
The vague and far restlessness of the distant sea,
Hills which are but a green, petrified
Magnification of yonder distant, quiet blue ocean,
Caught and calcified when blown, long ago,
Into roaring walls by rebellious breezes,
Caught, and no longer shifting currents of
Uncertain liquid, but adamantine,
Once a Peter before the cock
Now the corner stone, the Pontifex,
Greened over rock and with trees tufted,
Shifted with shrub, sheering away
In a hawk swoop to the unseen
Whisperings of the vague valley,
Everlasting hills, obedient hills,
Once more here I bow before you,
But not alone.

Bow before you, and close up dark
My eyes, and wax-block my ears
Lest I look long at the crow-sweeps of your crests,
Or hear the sea-reminiscent whispers
Which attendant breezes send up through
The valley and round the slopes.

For how dares this I call 'I'
This foul clay, this clot,
Look, hear and force foot upon your matted bracken?
Well that your far stretches I touch only with mine eyes
And soil not with my hands!

II

Soft, sunset clouds, now with feline deftness drifting,
Relentless as the new leaves of Spring,
On the East side here, quite coloured,
Not dripped in dyes as your Western brothers,
Sunset clouds, 'puff-balls' swinging slowly on
And away to the darkness of Night,
Once more here I bow before you,
But not alone.

III

Everlasting hills and sunset clouds,
You I cannot touch with hands,
Yet her who stands beside me.

IV

Moulder of mountains, God!
Who shepherds these clouds along,
Who hand-squirmed mud of her
Now here beside me,
You wonder not at warm eyes blurred
When strong mountains brace
And soft clouds shelter,
And your own image, in a pure
Clay-transmuting body, love
This clay, this clot, this I call 'I'.

FOR THOMAS AQUINAS

Once and for all, Thomas, you made the choice
Refused the fleshy toy with sizzling brand,
Your knowing mother could just understand
The refusal and acceptance in your voice
The rebellious "no" that is not negative the clois-
tered "yes" that draws the roses from the sand
The eyes upon the post, upon the plough the hand
Thrusting past the poppy's opiate voice.

Ah siren blooms, ah flesh inviting love,
God-made, but teaching us to temporise
Unless we, like Thomas, see but do not touch,
Our restless soaring closing its wings above
The only furrow we can fertilize,
We having made the choice to do as much.

IN THE DANCE HALL
for groups of men and women

W. I am a nurse I cannot catch disease.
I am a factory hand, the law protects me from
Undue exposure to cutting blades,
To grinding wheels, to white heat and
To falling iron. Our work is safe.

M. I am a clerk, I can hardly lose my job.
I walk the floors in safety, of a certain shop,
The prices marked, the sizes shown,
I seek advice on cheques by calling in
The manager. Our work is safe.

W. & M. But we are male and female, making and
Accepting invitations to the dance.
We cross the Atlantic when the band
Strikes up; crossing we're accepted and refused:

Accepted as a risk, refused as safe;
We manage to confuse our quest
At times with the urgings of the race;
And boredom drives us to the bored.

W. We're bored with waiting to be asked,
We dance together then; we hope sometimes
Two men would spare our being unmasked,
Would cease their hesitation to the dance.

M. We hoped you would not seem so eager;
Although we want to sail those seas
We have no port in mind, no haven;
We'll trust to rocking wave and music breeze.

W. Your arms must steady us upon
This rise and fall of dreams,
Your arms must steady us afloat
This ocean's secret streams.

M. & W. Strike up, strike up, the magic band,—
We'll risk the voyage across the floor,
Leave the safety-seekers on the sand,
Hasten from coastal quiet to mid deep's roar.

A PRAYER
For D.G.M.A.F.

I have loved the beauty of thy house, Lord,
And the place where thy glory dwells:
And the black diamond night which you gently twirl
Till every facet shines a star;
The lignum vitae, gold of fruit
And blue of bud;
The everlasting sea with its diurnal heaving,
Breathing, sighing and at night its whispered tales
And meteor trails where the fast fish stirs
The phosphorus:
The place where thy glory dwells.

Lord, I have loved the beauty of thy house
Whom you shaped from clay like mine,
In whose brown, flashing eyes and small woman body
You dwell, the Maker, the Owner
Of her whose — how can it be! whose
For-you-keeper I am.

THE FACADE OF THE EGLISE DE BROU

The birds that sing
the birds that fly
are birds that live
and birds that die.

The men who build
the men who break
the simple arc

construct in stone
what men alone
of animals remark:

the straight assault
too simply makes
the point, and fades.

The twist constructs
the cloth that lasts.
The jaguar arc,

efficient to a fault,
is animal;
direct, deadly and
ephemeral.

IGNORING HURTS

My breasts are dry
and long for love
Do not be shy
and long for love
My breasts are dry
and long for love
Enfold caress
do not be shy
I'll only bless
I long for love
My breasts are dry
enfold caress
Bite if you must,
ignoring hurts
I am as dust
that waits the call
My breasts are dry
and long for love
Do not pass by
but softly smooth
The wrinkles out
and gently touch
That I can shout
my breasts are dry
But need not long
need not (gently!)
Need not long
(and firmly smooth
The wrinkles out!)
and need not long
(And gently touch
and press and tear
Caress!) and need
not long for love,
And need not long—
ignoring hurts.

ON SEEING THE REFLECTION OF NOTRE DAME IN THE SEINE

For Louis Arnaud Reid

A man builds better than he knows
The cathedral, stone before floodlight's invention
Through floodlight's shimmering reflection
On matted water long after renews perfection
A man builds better than he knows

What he seeks is not hereafter
But everlasting now well done
The answer in stone or images
Built for the now that is forever
With every invention finds further perfection

He makes the poem, the cathedral
The image, the tune, the stone
So sweetly stretched the tension—
That is perfection — in stone
He cut's stone's dreams, and the world's and his

A man builds better than he knows.

A poet at the crossroads
In a strange land,
Caught by his long forgotten song
As it falls from a curtained window,
Suddenly hears it as I see
This night's reflection
Steady in the moving stream
Knowing that he builds well
Who builds better than he knows.

May 1960

II: UTOPIA

WHEN OTHER HEARTS AND OTHER LIPS

Grand Ma, from far away
you're not my real
grandma and your hair
is funny. But you're my best grandma, Grand Ma.

She, having no children
is called *Grandma* by strangers.

Her laughter once lighted up the dawn
yet her smile would hesitate:
she felt it forward to expect
a cloudless day.

And in the end when he was sent away
her smile, unquenched, hurt
our hearts and kept hope licking
at greenstick embers.

> *Oh screw them, says the lover now;*
> *I joined the RAF to die.*
> *They decorated me: I married*
> *a white woman as they wished.*
> *Tough tits on her whom I don't quite hate.*
> *D F C and bar — for bravery.*

The boy showed no spunk, the father said.
He could have eloped with the sow.

Knew an excellent Coloured once
from Kenya.
But mixed blood from Panama!

Grand Ma, from far away
you're not my real
grandma and your hair
is funny. But you're my best grandma, Grand Ma.

She nods remembering
how her smile lifted-in the dawn,
a dawn without a day.

That smile lights up a wrinkled face,
a face that outstared love and hate,

and still, when evening shadows
disguise the crunching snow,
can call up flashing fire
to keep cold sweat at bay.

Grand Ma, from far away
you're not my real
Grandma and your hair
is funny. But you're my best grandma, Grand Ma.

THIS TREE MY TIME KEEPER

is brown with berries now.

When last I looked it had
no leaves, was stiff and white
with frost.

Now green leaves and brown berries toss,
toss and bob in the whipping wind.

It is not Spring beyond the horizon
that the bucking boat is heading for,

"It is not Spring with its false hopes,
it is not Spring," says my time keeper,

"but bitter berries, bitter and brown
and full of wisdom."

Only in hard winters, they tell me
will the birds touch these berries.

WEDDING LONG AGO AND FAR AWAY

Here we come gathering
nuts in May, nuts in May
on cold and frosty mornings

a cup of tea and slice of bread
a cup of tea and slice of bread

on cold and frosty mornings.

At Louise's wedding in Jamaica
we played those games, played those
games at Louise's wedding.

and here we chop off your head
and here we chop off your head.

In Jamaica what to make
of cold and frosty mornings?
In Jamaica what to take
with cup of tea and slice of bread,

and London Bridge was falling
falling down so merrilee,
at a wedding falling down,
falling down so merrilee.

and when they 'chopped off your head'
you fell on the family carpet
beneath the star-apple tree,
a captive pressed for tug-of-war.

I stepped on Louise's gown
as she sailed up the aisle,
my fellow page and I
distracted as we carried her train.

a cup of tea and slice of toast
on frosty English mornings
can't match cousin Louise's style
gliding along the sacred coast

of controversial matrimony.

Games they say prepare us
for adult life. Like London Bridge
is falling down, falling down

and here we chop off your head
chop off your head on cold
and frosty mornings.

                                        And what
of starapple tree, and carpet
stage-set for games and guests
fixed on a saffron afternoon —

all our tropical patrimony?

We live abroad, and gather moisture
in May, beneath a milky moon.

IN AUTUMN ONE THINKS OF SILENCE

The leaves of France are calling me
leaves that speak with tongues of fire,
the tiny crests of yellow leap
about the skirts of green and higher
the rolling red engulfs the keep
of hills and thinning trees. An invisible sea
weaves purple on the forest floors
and rushing through the valley doors
lights up with rainbow lamps the wandering way.

At night bird-song and stars in trees
that lean across the cliff-wall of the seas,
dark seas opaque to the silver moon
that rising early, sinks too soon.

The birds that shine, the stars that sing in trees
bring sleep to weary souls who need their dreams.

The seething sea that covered, and covers, all
transmits through Autumn leaves, and my grey hair, a call
louder than trees leaning with the turning year
as Earth corners through its universal sphere,

calling us from France and fiery leaves
and ocean deep-shadowed or dreamy grey,
to the confines of those who stay
unspeaking, where silent stars in consort weave

and waiting angels stream
their light along the Way.

FOR NELSON MANDELA

It is easy and
Impertinent to call you
Brother. I sit fussing,
You locked in jail
Banned and unquotable
At sixty years of life
In death by accident of
Birth. Ah, Nelson, not
Blind in any eye
Know that you are
Remembered far beyond
The tyrants that hold you
Still.

August 1980

I WATCH THE LIGHT RETURN

I watch the light return
And objects growing whole
The inverted L of light
Becomes a square a door

A door through which the world
Returns the world of squares
Of shapes that hold their form
That hold my mind in shape

The shape of things
When light returns to show
The tables chairs and trees
That in my dreams dissolve

I slip and slide at night
I bilocate across
The globe and time I bend
Iron and trees to fly

Me gently through the years
At whiff of sherry or
Of dying coals beneath
The christmas cooking in the yard

The light returns informing all
Shapes with relief relive
Their green and daily forms
The common round alas

Is where we are and where
We will be until the light
That blinds shall wake us to
The endless song not heard

Because so sweet and real
The song between the song
And silence singing through
The light and dark between

The dawn and after dawn
The firmness of the shape
Without the shape the form
That does not need the form

Astride vibrating waves
Of flesh or blood or seas
The light returns from dreams
No longer light alone

Floating assures release
In water the body is
And is not torn apart
By seas still holding firm

The door is more than door
The window chairs and trees
Are firm and loose and more
The light returns from dreams

El Centro and St. Thomas, May-June 1974

TWO FROM CIDRA

For John Peter Hawes

I

This house frames our way of viewing
As where we live is always doing
How we our dwellings choose
To ensure they shape our views!

II

The grass grows the cows eat it
C'est la Vie as some people meet it

SPRING HAS COME

Spring has come
(Pale green leaves)
as I breathe
their new scent
fields of grass
eyeing light
pressing blue
I feel death

I feel death
blossoms fall
grasp their white
scattered on
violets
green leaves up
skies of trust
Spring has come

Spring has come
(pale green leaves)
as I breathe
their new scent
fields of grass
eyeing light
pressing blue
I feel death

I feel death
blossoms fall
grasp their white
scattered on
violets
green leaves up
skies of trust
Spring has come

Spring has come
(pale green leaves)
as I breathe
their new scent
fields of grass
eyeing light
pressing blue
I feel death

I feel death
blossoms fall
grasp their white
scattered on
violets
green leaves up
skies of trust
Spring has come

THE PETALS OF THE ROSE

The petals of the rose
I tore methodically
One by one unfurling
The tight pink ball
A gentle fragrance
Oozed from the bruised leaves
The tight and smooth curling
Had annoyed me.

What is whole is hard
On man
What is torn does not
Suffice.

The rose petals are in the dust
The rose bud broken
But not for seeding.

Yet in the mind
Long after pink has bruised
To brown
A lasting blossom rises
Steady with a fragrance all
Its own:
"What is whole is hard
On man
What is torn does not suffice"

LACRYMAE RERUM

Sunt
        leave the latin alone
                        lacrymae

things are full of tears
        for what cause
                        rerum

cognoscere
        for what cause

who knows

but that tears are
        too deep in things

            Jerusalem came upon him
                around a dusty turn
Jerusalem   Jerusalem my people

            and Jesus wept

Lovely beauty in sunlight glows
        and in sunlight fades

            the cream yellows

and green stiffens to brown
            silk to crackle

            I watched the moonlight
from a height in St. Vincent

the womb-like curve of the coast
receiving the unheard roll
of the waves

and the thick creamy neads
formed and reformed

They bunched up and spread out
and disappeared and bunched up
and spread out
and disappeared

the moon the persistent stars
the heaving cream in the bend of the bay

and the tears as salt as the sea
and the tears as salt as the sea

the harsh rum
the harsher steel

were soft at the top of that hill
and the unheard sough of the sea spoke of

lacrymae rerum

a solo voice at midnight mass
belcantoing an out-worn hymn
reopening the incision

that should have cut off childhood
and memories of a father lately dead
the cause

of tears
cognate
constant confused
but there
in the breaking of a coffee pot
or the holding so close in the dance
or in the proposition meant
and not meant
accepted and refused

or in the birth
or leaving bed

in orange evening
or silver dawn
there is something about Troy
Jerusalem St. Vincent

about a child losing
his books or bus-fare

the old man hearing the news

the hardly contained girl
bursting with sap

hurrying never to hear
from some battle-front
or camp after camp after camp

if you press too hard
if you push too soon
if you wait too long

if . . . . .
  always
    now
    or then

things are full of tears

SPANISH DANCER IN NEW YORK

"But so simple" said the dear
All American gal who couldn't screw
                                        not really
She *had* slept with twenty men
By the end of college
                                        or soon thereafter
Without satisfying any of them
                                        or herself

But she declared
The deeply damask skin
And shimmering jelly of the Spanish loins
                                        rather simple
A trick too easily won,

No pirouettes of reason there
                                        apparently
And certainly no chatter
About problems and adjustments
And our national posture
No presentation there, my dear,
Of anything that could be remotely called
                                        relevant

But, perhaps, some food
                                        for thought?

THE LITTLE BOY AT DAWN

For Ralph and Dody Thompson

The little boy at dawn

In his night gown,
His fibrous sun
The mango in his hand.

Open the world and sweet
Ripe "Number Eleven"!

"Where is the boy?"

Lost like his son like his
Mother who looked that morning.
Lost like discarded fruit
Bitten once, twice and cast aside.

The yellow images remain
The pungent world gazed at
From leaning head, hopeful.

But lost the boy, the mango and the man.

BIRTHDAY POEM 1970

The summer that brings me
My fiftieth year
Brings me also
Yet another unfinished poem
A certificate of merit
Or two
No silver gold nor bronze

Fifty years of not quite
Gaining anything
(But weight
And a chance of understanding
What it means to
Be nearly third
Best, regularly)

Curacao August 4, 1970

STRAIGHT EDGES BREAK

For Aubrey Williams

Straight edges break
Straight edges break into
Into outer space
Straight edges break

The sea's edges break
Break into probes
Into the spread ellipses
Like constant lace
Like constant lace riding
The thighs of the bronzed
Horsewoman rocking rocking

Up the edges the sea horses
Climb like agile fingers
Probing until the rock shudders

Straight edges break
Away from cubes and pyramids
Like fire like fire
The edges break
The edges break into
The fire that I and edges share

Break into the fire
That white and smooth
Probes these rocks and those
Outer spaces probes
My inner fire solid fuel
Shifting its edges

The straight edge breaks into
The straight edge breaks
The straight edge of
The girl dancing edges
Nearer her partner and then breaks

Breaks into shattering motion
Like the fire of the sea
Around its granite blocks

The sea breaks
The sea breaks into
The sea recovers herself and pauses
Like the fire of the girl
Holding her arms to herself

Before and after dancing

Centro Caribeno, May 1975

OH WHEN IN GREEN FIELDS

Oh when in green fields I have recalled thy
Beauty, love, when the rounded furrows imitate
Thy breasts and silent pines thy posture
Oh earth cannot be separate from thee
Nor stars that cluster round the stems of night:
The landscape takes thy many shapes without
Thy sublety and has no rivers deep
As thy mysterious waters.

One flesh with mine oh even here amidst
The German tongues and silent pines thy breasts
Are indivisible from me and thy dancing limbs,
And that essential oceanic plasmic element
Our love the blood that makes our cleaving to
Alive that drowns our single-cellular
  Reactibility into leaping births
  Of blood and sea.

FOR DANNY WILLIAMS

Cassava and plantains
Nourished you.

Now your body nourishes them.
Your bones will build
For unsuspecting youths
Bodies as coo-coo built yours.

Your poems gentle in your way
Seeped through our foo-foo stuffed bodies
Enlightening them. They will lift
Our youth quietly to see our skies.

Goodbye, Danny, goodbye;
Still "the clouds are a flock of sheep
Grazing over the fertile vault".

Still our human bodies
Turn plantains and cassava
Into love and poetry.

Walk good, Danny, walk good
We walk with you, Danny
We walk with death.

"The uncertain seine, a bundle of nerves,
molests the sad sand"

We walk with you, Danny,

We walk with life

Carifesta, Guyana, 1972

THE DESCENT TO WATER

Y la caballería
A vista de las aguas descendía
San Juan de la Cruz: *Canciones entre el alma y el Esposo*

And the horses
Seeing the water
Descended

From brown red dust
And harsh bites of erosion
Through green declines

The horses
Seeing the water
Descended
Stretching veined necks
And white tongues.

Up long throats
The water works its way
Rippling brown
Dusty flesh

The men
Roll over on the grass
Feeling earth
Like green wool give
And take, welcome
And withhold
Burrowing their itching
Shoulders

Grasping the green
Pulling knees up
To their chests pressing
On mother earth
An embrace that
Held them now and would
Forever hold them after.

From distance where
Water floated blue
And nearer shone like silver
The remnant had
Slowly descended

From rusty nails
Of orange and yellow
Broken columns of rock
To the water's gracious edging
Of the green.

Now slowly through their bones
They feel how the crystal flow
That softens stones
And rocks
So sweetly feeds the green

So long they had not seen
Bubbles breaking round the rocks
Had been dry
Had not heard the spirit
Whispering in the waters
Rushing by.

COSMOPOLITAN PIG

For George Lamming

Nihil alienum mihi humanum est
or
"Man 'top yu 'tupidness."

The minds of all men are similar in their feelings and operations, nor can any one be actuated by any affection, of which all others are not, in some degree, susceptible.
David Hume, *Treatise*, pp. 575-6.

A sculptured poem
Or long-lined church
Clean the line with rhymes
That chime but hardly show,
The poem in another language
From another time,
The church at Brou
Geometry in stone
Or at Les Baux
Outcrop of bauxite soil
Before that earth became
Red mother of metal,

Irrelevant to those
Who hate to see
Beyond the dust beneath their feet
Who dare not look within
Lest they find dreams
That stretch across the earth
Like air
Sympathies covering the globe
More urgent than missiles
Festering with hate.

The stone I break from Carib hills
To make a pot or build a church
Binds me to Pyramids
And megoliths in Egypt or Peru
The church I love at Brou
Is part of that
Geometry of the sea
That rolls upon itself
In blues and greens
At Tower Isle
Or solidifies in whites
About the Crane.

What is Barbados, or Peru
Provence or Rome
But places which Any Man
Can make their home?

Home is too human
Work, making, building
Too much a part of us
To be particular

No sharp stroke shaping stone
No bend of metal or curve
Of well-kept hill
No plotted field of cane
Or wheat or rice;
No garden by the railroad
Or formal as the French
No Ife bronze
Or illuminated script
Is alien to me.

WINTER NIGHT

From my window I could see
That silver ice had bent the birch
And forced it, cross-beam wise, to lurch
Against a coal-black tree.

On the hearth, as on a perch,
Sparrows of russet flame
Leapt in an aery game
As vigil lights in a midnight church.

A black gust shrieked its wrath,
The white birch, falling, sighed,
The sparrows gasped, then died
And left their grey ash cold upon the hearth.

YES, I RECALL

Yes, I recall the sudden forsythia
Of early Spring
And white tunes, overwrought,
When snowflakes used to sing.

And in my dreams, the pines
I used to know
Still daub with shadows
The moon-blue snow.

GIRL IN THE MOONLIGHT

I turned the steep corner and there she sat
In the moonlight on the ledge,
Her head against the skies and over the edge
of that rocky bench her legs dangling.
She looked to the valley, sometime flooded,
Now filled with moonlight, to the skies, where wrangling,
Crows fly by day and tonight the quiet clouds.

She sat there alone and seemed to bare
Her face to the moonlight and the breeze.
What girl is this, I thought,
Ledge-seated, alone, on the hill top above the trees?

Is she as pure as the cloud-foam of the skies
Which the good ship moon has ruffled up?
As the stream that in the valley lies,
Carefree? Is it longing that bring her out
Alone, alone against the skies:
Or having too much what others seek
Does she look for surcease here
Alone in the moonlight on the peak?

The heart that loves this heart that throbs
In time with songs of crickets and of frogs
Is probably pumping blood into the sea
Where the sunken freighter has left its logs
And a longed for head that bobs
Or like the birds that in feed-time fly
Through this valley in search of a resting place
Has her heart soared only above the dry
And yellow grass and rests tonight in dreams
Of rain tomorrow and a green watering place?

Yet, picture-framed by clouds against moon and stars,
Hair flowing from the upright head,
This girl, frozen thus for memory by one quick glance
To me is dead, is dead, is dead:

No use to probe the secrets of the scars.

The heart might open for as long as a meteor glides
Then it clamps closed, rigid as a dead crab's claw,
And the trailing glory is gone
And the stars that began to swim
Are stony-fixed.

As earth through every tree,
From base to leaf-top, through every forked branch
And veined leaf stretches for the sun,
So heart for heart.

And when the heart-sun arises
There is sap-thrill:
And when the heart-sun sinks in the night-sea
There is sap-clot:
And in the heart-year
All days are short,
All nights,
Long.

She sits there ever, beyond my reach,
Alone on the hill-top by night,
By day in the crowded valley alone,
Save in the sharp coming of some short dawn;
Or when in an eye's flash,
The cloud veil rent,
The naked sun speaks to the trees.

OEDIPUS AT COLONUS

I come to these mountains
I Oedipus though blind
Can see the tops gently
Touched with white the dawn blue
As clean as my purged self
I come at dawn to wait for dusk.

When the life-giver has warmed
Away the silver lace of dew
And warmed this sacred grove
After noon he will withdraw
Beneath the crisp whiteness
Of the round mountain in the west there
The cooling grove shall darken
And grow secret
I shall follow him into the dusk
Below the peak.

Daughters, when the sun and your father
Leave you in saffron shadows
Consider my life's day-tramp here
Seek not yet to know what night brings.

SONG

Eva, Eva some lost blonde world
Eva, Eva, in the spring, in the rain,
        on the wing, at rest
Eva a symbol clear solid light of the best
We could have dreamt of or fashioned.

Oh God to see her a draped statue on
        arm of a chair,
Leaning forward overflowing, waiting to speak.
How couldst thou have made her so fair
And a poor man so weak!

HOW LATE, HOW LATE . . .

How late, how late, September Spring
You touch and startle my unquiet
Heart with green and brown that fling
Their charms, as cool as Autumn clouds,
Yet warming, hard against the blue
That left me cold when lambs were leaping.

Hoary Winter held in keeping,
Though he had died, my heart; my heart
You must not wring so, jung frau,
In muslin white, with eyes that brown
The light that shines too bright within.

How late, how late, September Spring.

Through the burgeoning of Spring
I slept and through Summer's heat
I have avoided ocean's foam
And golden fields so perfumed at
The touch of Aphrodite's feet.

Now you with early brown
And later blue have come
To set my heart aquiver where
It hangs upon an Autumn tree.

How late, how late, September Spring.

England, 1952

THE GARDEN, GREEN AND GREAT

For A.C.

The garden, green and great,
A park dark shadowed
By tall tamarinds
By guangoes' multiple
Delicate leaves balanced
On every wind against the sun.

The sun-light lances through
Only to a pond, the pond
In the centre, resting skies
And clouds on her bosom
Reflecting them
To shaded grass where I stand.

The green shadows of tall
Trees fall on edges of pond.
As mauve blossoms float down
To perfect water, they
Live twice: in air floating,
And imaged on water.
Then when the blossom meets its calm
Image on smooth water
All is lost
(Soon the pool resmooths
Its green grimace.)

Around the pond are sweet bowers
Around the bowers green grasses
Flecked with mauve and yellow blossoms;
Red hibiscus, yellow
Allamanda, purple bougainvillea
Surround and dome the bowers.

In each lives a lady with her maid:
A delicate Chinese with almond eyes and yaourt skin;
A tall black girl whose skin shines—
And her eyes—like a starry night;
A bowl of cream and cherries is
The face of the white Juno there;
And with a glitter and a tinkle glides
The golden sari and black-bird blackness
Of the Indian's hair.

The blossoms keep falling gently
On the grass, gently on the pool,
But more heavily spoiling all.

When the yellow moon drips its butter
Over all, I sit and breathe
Jasmine, orange blossom, quick-stick;

The yellow moon climbs out of trees
And in open sky above the central pond
Is burnished silver, and phosphorescent green.

I lean over the bank
And wonder at my reflection in the water;
A smile arises from the depths
And spreads over the surface,
I see myself in the centre of that smile;
I hear nothing, I dream of
The almond eyes, the black skin,
The black hair, the blood
Beneath the cheeks.

Walking over blossomed grass,
A bell disturbs me, I follow.
Up a silver glade,
Black, bucking at shadows
Tossing his pointed horns
Into the soft butter
Of the moonlight snorts
A tense unquiet bull,
Escaped from a nearby farm.

AT HOME THE GREEN REMAINS

In England now I hear the window shake
And see beyond its astigmatic pane
Against black limbs Autumn's yellow stain
Splashed about tree-tops and wet beneath the rake.

New England's hills are flattened as crimson-lake
And purple columns, all that now remain
Of trees, stand forward as hillocks do in rain,
And up the hillside ruined temples make.

At home the green remains: the palm throws back
Its head and breathes above the still blue sea,
The separate hills are lost in common blue
Only the splendid poinsettias, true
And crimson like the northern ivy, tack,
But late, the yearly notice to a tree.

England, 1948

III: ARS LONGA

NOTRE DAME DE CHARTRES
Variations on a Theme by Charles Peguy

You appear, longed for Chartres,
an arrow at the sky, far yet near,
no ancient oak but solid hope upon
the farthest strand, a pilgrim's
final mount and perfect sphere,

Mona Lisa of the plains,
floating at far horizon's edge
above the wool of harvest and of woods.

Uncertain captive of your smile,
my pilgrim thirst ascends
and again is slaked in your
precise transparencies.

Higher than all your saints

greater than any king,

you shake the sunlight on your feet,

unfaulted spires that never fail.

THE WINGED VICTORY OF SAMOTHRACE

Her toes upon the boat
Upon my breath her wings
The lightness of her touch
Before the earth she swings
Her hips aslant, her drapes
Where she had hovered float
Relaxed she does not clutch
The dried up earth where live
The stinking weeds and grapes
Are wizened with long war

A victory may hover
In stasis pure and still
But peace takes years to kill
The cancerous hate-lover
Time it took to form
(Between descent and climb)
A head (now lost) an arm
All that grew so warm
With vision and with care

Which can together give
To stone or man or place
This gentle touch to calm
The fragile ship of time
This solid lift to space.

BROU, PHILIBERT LE BEAU I.

Take a bit of well-baked, light, golden well knit, smooth grained corn cake; place it in a silver plate, a plate deep and shaped like a stylised fish, a flat, longish balanced fish; let the corn cake rest, and pour, not on it but beside it, into the well shaped silver platter, a rich but clear sauce, the colour of yellow chartreuse, but with the slightest touch of rose in it, the very slightest touch of the rosy first light of day on a cool tropical morning. The sauce must be rich, but not viscous; golden-rose; clear but not thin. Slowly the corn cake will absorb it; the corn cake will remain firm but its yellow pulp and brown rind will be completed, softened, enriched by the absorbed liquid. So stands the church at Brou, built by Margaret of Austria for Philibert le Beau, when between 11 in the morning and early afternoon it takes to itself the firm, rich golden sunlight, and absorbs it, softens it, enriches it, and with its carved fruits, and oft repeated initials of P le B, makes the sunlight part of it, and in so doing manages to suggest a slightly rosy sky, or the palest of rose petals.

BROU, PHILIBERT LE BEAU II

Choose golden, well-knit, smooth-grained corn cake,
  Place it in a silver plate, shaped like a stylised fish,
Let the corn cake rest, and pour, not on but beside it,
  a clear rich sauce,
    the colour of yellow chartreuse,

Golden, rose-clear, but not thin;
  The brown rind is enriched
    By this liquid
  The yellow pulp completed.

So stands the church at Brou,
Built by Margaret of Austria for Philibert le Beau,
When between morning and fore-noon
  It takes to itself the gold sunlight,
Absorbs it, softens, enriches it, and with
      carven fruit,
And the often repeated initials
  of P le B, P le B,
Makes sunlight a part of it:
  Carved sky of dawn,
  Palest of rose petals.

ON HEARING DVORAK'S "NEW WORLD" SYMPHONY

The chestnut trunks are dark
Their massive manes are green
And lightly float on dark
Breathing of music wind.

The white swans sail the pond
Before the music wind,
And arch white necks among
The waving chestnut trees.

The music wind billows,
The dark trunks toss green manes:
The swans have felt darkness
Weave slowly through the waves.

I am kneeling in
A nightfall church beyond
The rings of candle light
Which shake in music wind.

One by one acolytes
Are candles leaving dark
The altar whose candles
One by one flicker out.

The nightfall church is night
Except for sanctuary lamp;
I taste the lamp and know
The song of music wind.

Outside, the church of night
Glows with sanctuary lamps.
As music wind falls off
The quiet pond is bright,

No swans, no ducks, no waves
Of green rippling water;
Only quiet stars
Like clouds lighted by dawn,

Like flowers lighted by Spring;
Only bright stars weaved in
The still pond; the song
Of music makes a silence.

THE WHITE THE GREEN AND THE RED (AFTER HORACE'S SORACTE ODE)

For Derek Walcott

See how Soracte glistens white
Above brown branches bending low
Where streams stand stiff and grey

Cherish the fading logs
Within the womb-like fire place
While their winter light leaps
To life in this red wine moving
Slowly round our Zodiac

Full flavour on the tongue
Closed eyes upon the inner self—

Wild winds beat up black waters
At times they twist, at times they stroke
The ancient ash and quiet cypress.

What tomorrow will bring forget,
Should the wheel spin extra days
Rejoice! The dance and love and song
Are now, before white bones
Begin their endless creak.

The corners of the Park are green
And, through the dark, hissing voices
And knowing laughter reveal
How snatched at fingers yield
Their favours in struggles
Not pointlessly prolonged.

THE SPRING AND THE STREAM

The spring and the stream
Variations upon a theme:
O Fons Badusiae splendidior vitro....
Spring of Bandusia, crystal clear....
Horace *Carm. III-13.*

I'll kill the kid before
He learns to mount and buck

I'll pour his blood with wine
And roses in your crystal stream

What clarity has not, red stains supply.

His budding horns are washed
Away by your cool water

Warmed with young blood and roses
Your voice through mine will rise
And rising rule loquacious streams.

II

The quiet ox stares at
Your shining waters, cool
And crystal clear

Wine and roses
I'll give you, and blood
Flowing from the vain wrangler

Whose budding horns
Will never know love or war.

The dog days have been watered by you
And tired bulls and wandering flocks;

My gifts will place your voice
Among the famous fountains

As your waters run red
Beneath the oak, through hollow rocks.

III

Your waters that cool the wandering ox
Will be warmed by young red blood

I'll have your chattering voices
Heard above the sounds of other streams

Tomorrow I'll sacrifice to you
The budding fronds and yearnings

Of the too lively goat whose male
Blood (with folded roses) will

Tinge your so limpid stream.

Mona/Cidra 1971

LA TABERNA, (AFTER LORCA)

For Robert Gilkey

I

Death
Comes and goes
In the tavern

Black horses pass
And ugly folk
Through dark passages
Of the guitar

A brackish whiff
And menstrual
Mixes with the tuber roses
From the beach

Death
Comes and goes
Goes and comes
In the tavern

II

"Do you ever hear of Bob?"
I read in your round hand
Above that Lorca Poem

Death living in
The tavern
Coming in and going out
And black horses champing
With their ugly folk
In the dark passages of the guitar

And the brackish whiff
Mixed with too much tuber rose
Of menstrual blood
And fetid beach.

III

Do you ever hear of Bob?

Around you then
Clung the crisp aroma
Of pine needles in
The sun
The soft sweetness of
Lactation although
You were so virginal
You were so soft
Gentler rose
Entering leaving
To cadenzas of the harp

Our life

The tavern.

FOR, AND AFTER SAPPHO

Sappho, the sea suggests
Aphrodite
You don't mind
Do you?

The sea excites
Like strong soft woman
Excites and threatens

The sound of the sea
Makes me
Nervous

Trees grow
Seas last
Trees hope
The sea remains
For a while
Trees seem sturdy
The sea troubled

Only the strong
And soft
Have faith
With your two arms
You can
Touch
the sky

HESPERA (AFTER SAPPHO)

Evening, you bring together
All that bright dawn scattered
You bring home the sheep
You bring home the goat
The child you bring home
To his mother

TRANSLATION FROM HORACE, ODES, Bk. II, 14

Dismal Cocytos
Wandering, faintly flowing,
And the notorious race of Danaus,
And Sisyphus condemned to endless labour,
You must visit.

You must leave your soil, your home
Your ever pleasing wife,
Your tended trees, no not one of them
Save the hated cypress
Will follow you, their brief master.

Your worthy heir will drink up the Caecuban
Guarded now by a hundred keys, tainting
The tiles with that proud wine,
At more than priestly feasts.

FROM HORACE, ODES I, 5
TO PYRRHA

Who is the green-horn with you now,
Pyrrha, in the long grass by the garden wall?
Is he urgent in his tweeds as he presses
His cheek on the "natural tint" of your golden hair?

When his green gods fade, on some
Dark sea he will weep
And wonder at the black winds
And bitter waves—his faith
Now teaches him that you are always golden
Always green spring and lovable.

Oh the poor men who think you so fresh!
My shipwreck was nearly fatal
But the gods who saved me
Have received on their temple walls
My soaking tweeds for a thanksgiving.

BROU III

In Memoriam John Cunneen

Grey and rust

and gently pink against the blue
but no one stops
and no one stops
and no one stops to think of you

The light is fading
the virgins pass
the young are full of juice
like a slice of endless time
you face the fading sun
the cruel cross is marked on you
your windows pattern endlessly
the sorrow to something new
you stand so clean
you are not seen

And no one stops
and no one stops
and no one stops to think of you

The thighs that pass are firm
the faces dull
they cannot notice you
your whisper is so light
you are so still
you are so still

that no one stops to think of you

Just before night the light whitens
in different planes you stand
but no one stops

Three upright planes
  where late but one
  as light lessens improving sight

the geometry of your windows
  of your looped facades
  of your whole self
measures the earth
    and sorrow's faith

you stand a well worked sign

    and no one stops
    and no one stops
    and no one stops to think of you

Your endless geometry is sure and calm
built on a love-match that did
not seem to last

O your quiet speaks across the roar
and stink of diesel engines
and faint aroma of aperitifs
it speaks it sings it soothes
for one building
in grey and rust

    a hope

IV: VITA BREVIS

BUILDING INCOMPLETE

Never able to build an innings or
a house; applauded strokes at times;
a room, a wall, a verse well shaped.

But is that all?

Spires standing by themselves?
shapely columns holding
up skies and dreaming clouds?

A single rose against
a northern wall,
alone he stood admiring it.
He'd grown so small

remembering the promise,
not only of the rose
which burst so soon
through hardened clay ....

Never able to build an innings or
a house, his garden shows
a pleasant shade or two,
a doorless vacant stall
a green strand here, and there a brown,

where knowing bushes frown
as they stand in line
to greet the glowing rose
eloquent by the garden wall.

ON LOSING GRIP...

Like white sand slipping through
the fingers of a child,
the stars, the world and poems
elude me relentlessly,
galaxies fading at dawn ...

  the budding
of the white rose
is done before I can dream it.
already its thorny branches are being burnt ...

It's not that every thing flows
and all processes, but the pageant moulds.

Before I raise my hands to shade my eyes
snow flakes melt and freeze to ice.

CLOSURE

Dear Albertine

my mother—do you remember her?—
explained when I asked why
old Mrs D'Costa grunted as she walked,

"It eases her."

Tall, steel-grey hair in a bun,
her loose white gown to her heels,
unbent but slow, she shuffled across
the lane to our house leaning on
a crooked stick. She grunted.

It eased her.

I was only seven when
she called out from gossiping
with my grand mother:

"Mr Pinto agreed that Ruthie
should marry young Lyons
because he brought his sister along
when he came courting—
remember that!"

That was not my style, you
know Albertine, when long ago
I went courting.

Now I grunt a lot.

It eases me.

EPITAPH

The old man is gone
            Him ded, sah, him ded!
(Where are the frigate birds?)

Absent from Jonkunoo Lounge,
Someone will miss him from
The Caribe Bar — but only long
After.
            Him ded, sah, him ded!

In Santiago de los Caballeros
(O Spanish men on horses!)
They will remember when
It is too late how lively he
Could be.
            Him ded, sah; se murió.

But Tavern on the Green
Will dance, and Tower Isle
And Myrtle Bank, so stupidly
Demolished,
            (Him done ded, sah)

And wherever for a moment or
A night he used to cast the spell
Against death with dancing
A spell that works and does
Not work,
            (Him ded, sah, him ded!)

A spell that did not last.

The frigate birds have soared away,
The hurricane clouds have left
The skies clean blue;
And in the silence he has danced
Away, away, across the bar.

Him no ded, sah?

IT'S A CHINA PINK MORNING

It's a China pink morning
hung from a withered tree.

The yellow sand stretches out
on its dusty bed, slowly
changing postures, whimpering.

Nemesis alone knows
how soon the fruit will fall

splattering the yellow sleeper
with dry, bone dry, splinters of pink.

PROBLEMS OF A WRITER WHO DOES NOT QUITE .....

For Derek Walcott, his brother Roddy, his mother Alix and after reading Helen Vendler's Review of Walcott in the New York Review of Books

Roddy broder, teacher Alix son,
Bwoy, you no hear wa de lady say?
Watch di pentameter ting, man.
Dat is white people play!

Wha de hell you read Homer —
A so him name? — fa!
Yu his from the horal tradition
And must deal wid calypso and reggae na!

Mek I advise yu boy
If yu trouble white people toy
Especially as yu win big prize an ting
Yu arse goin swing

Like metronome, yu'd say,
But a black bwoy should play
Widout dem mechanical aids
Full of rydhm like all true spades.

(Eh eh a since when yu tun black?
Yu note-book does say yu never did notice
Whedder the sore was black or white dat wear de poultice,
But de lady slap "black experience" in yu back!)

See what dat pentameter an' ESSAY do
Yu bwoy! Long time I school yu
To break
        up yu

Lines
        Lines
                Lines
Like dat black writer Poe, black like his raven

Bruck it
        up
           man   an' wid de drums
                                      de drums

De tinti
        nab   u
                    la
tion of de drums, de drums

Black bwoy black bwoy
                    black

Bwoy.

No more of the loud sounding sea
Or the disjecta membra
Homer, Horace are not, are not for you and me
Colonials with too high a diction
instead of simple drug addiction.

Roll that spliff and break it up!
The simple diction, the lower registers
Are quite enough for colonials

Even if they snatch prizes from
The new
                Imperialists.

MAURICIO IS DEAD

In Memoriam Mauricio Swadesh

Mauricio se murió
Mauricio el suave
  Among los Anglo-Saxones
          (he wrote)
  One does not speak of death
Pero en México
    en México
Death is among
    those interesting themes
    that keep alive
An evening's talk.

Se murió Mauricio
Mauricio el suave.

What have I said
That you'll remember friend
When they tell you I'm dead
What will you remember
What will you remember friend—
That in Anglo-Saxon countries
One does not speak of death?

Remember Mauricio
Mauricio el suave
Who in Jamaica broke
His journey to
Ask us ¿Que tal?
And left and died.

Perhaps even here in Lima
Among tambours,
Latinos and saffron dancers,

I should have let it pass
        held back the urge
Not dropped among foaming
Pisque sours and mutual friends
        Swadesh se murió

He too must have
Faced this problem
Often

                Among drum beats
                and taught whispers
                    of the guitar

Dying often,
As once again
(Hearing such news)
You and I have died

Before the final death.

WARM THE EVENING AND STILL

In Memoriam
Yvonne, youngest daughter of Ina Alexander

Warm the evening and still
fit for funerals

O youngest rose on pistil side
from Ina sprung
And marked by that blooming
to this blighted end
Your strength to give life
cankered to your death
With long flickers of pain
brightening burning
Blistering your young flesh
to this dark death

Warm the evening and still
fit for funerals

Here among the hymns
your mother loved
Sticky as at the grave of your
dried grand mother
With her tufts of facial hair
and her pouting chin
Stuck out to the other world
drooping like palms
And bread-fruit leaves
in another island
We pray for you and ourselves

It is a quiet evening
Such as you would have hated
in your restless youth

Warm the evening and still
        fit for funerals

With our heat and sweat
        and our closeness
To living death. I am away

        as usual
But stand on the same
        taste of earth
As all your dear family knew
        by sea by graves
In the brief grassy overcoming
        that couples all
Shivering through the loins the sun and heat
        the quickening

Warm the evening and still
        fit for funerals

'And your heart'—our heart Mother—
        'a sword of sorrow shall transfix'.

There is no moving that avoids
        no shield that blunts

From birth he too was starcrossed
        to suffering
A sign for the raising up (Simeon said)
        and falling down
Of many. The Mother gives birth
        to death, come heat
Come hail in Alps or atolls

Warm the evening and still
fit for funerals

Elen, Ina gone and now you
third generation
But Ann Marie your child remains
and living faith

Now may you dismiss us Lord
the pain is gone
The pain will come again
we have seen your glory
Swift snatches of birds at dawn

dismiss us Lord
Pain kills and pain quickens
and death shall die

Warm the evening and still
fit for funerals.

EPIPHANIES

I: *From the "Tower" Class Room at St. George's College, Jamaica, during target practice from shore to sea*

I have lifted my eyes above their heads
And looked across the green protecting arm
That dams and breaks atlantic dreads;
From class-room tower and our babel to calm
Of inner sea unruffled by the slightest foam,
To open sea's roughcast and blue-white charm.

The heard and unseen arc of the shell strikes home
The Moses staff causing from the sea to sprout
A court-yard fountain, if heaven be the dome
Of blue upon the salt blue drought
Of desert ocean that needed this white rose,
This cluster white of bamboo shoots that out
Of blue rock at the strike of Moses grows
And pauses at the balance point that makes
The shape, that holds the pattern's close.

The bamboo plumes outward, white and takes
Its shape forever rooted in this sleeping sea
The hurrying motion of innumerable flakes
Of white and blue from ocean's rock I see
As motionless and full, unhurried calm,
As balanced as permanent as a perfect tree.

I look back at their faces' slight alarm
And wide-eyed wonder at my wandering—
These children's balanced being to be the palm
That bends to every wind's imposturing!
Each searching eye is a murky pool
Slowly lighted by shafts of quivering
Laughter. We turn the pages and make the best of school.

II. *At Cette, from the cemetery where Paul Valery is buried*

I stand upon a Mediterranean slope
  And look beyond white grave-stones to the tight
  Stretching of green water, a silken rope
Played from the central deep to the edges white;
  Aside in sandals I see the striding flesh
  As through a yew tree breaks the light

Of lovers in their summer white above the mesh
  Of grass and sand and clay that will sift them yet
  To their dead brothers whom no winds refresh
For whom the rush and dash of waves beget
No dreams, no green urges yearning towards the sea.

  The heard and unseen words of Valery set
Off the fountain from his tomb, and we
  Become the balanced fountain; the hurrying
  Constellations of our blood, the plea

Of every urge is caught; the scurrying
  Is at the balance point; each fountain drop
  Is held in place; our inner worrying
Moves no more and yet we grow,and stop
  Caught in the crystal pattern's close
  In the tree, in Valery's voiced fountain top,

In bamboo-shoots and sea's drought-quenching rose.

III. *On his Grandmother's Death, news of which he received in Lans-en-Vercours*

Amidst this blue of skies and white of snows
  I read the note from occidental hills
  From where the slug-trailed custard-apple grows
And the bastard bombay mango daily fills
  Its olive skin with juices that attain
  The cycle's point of closure where fullness kills,
From where her trees so blindly know the gain
  That sunlight brings, that soil provides, I hear
  That she is dead.

        Vibration of tolling bell again
I feel, first felt with her at funeral
  Of Bishop O'Hare, the sapling I beneath her shade
  Not dreaming yet that time that made me tall
Would bend her to the earth and with its spade

  Plough her ashes back to bless the soil
  While her spirit's crystal fountain played
Above the roughcast ocean, above the toil
  Of lovers young who stride on grass that covers
  The bones and melted breasts where coil
Fingers and worms of their dead brothers.

  The dead sea fountain sings to me with still
  Persisting shape, Valery's perpetual motion hovers
In his voiced words shaping the silence on a hill
  Above the central sea;

      but you whose death
  Disturbs these snows, scorching cold eyes that fill
The soul with wonder and with salt, even without breath
  You live, not an impressed scent among yellow pages,
  Not conjured back by any reader's breath,

But fountain of your being plays against the rages
  Of time's raucous sea, the rose you were and are
  And ever will be is your self still bursting through the ages.

THE GRAVE-DIGGER

(Written Holy Week 1947 at Paul Valery's grave in Cette on the Mediterranean, after listening to a reading of his verse)

At left white foam proliferates;
Its roots in sea, its boughs
Against the rocks and over them.

On the right oh the Mediterranean blue!
The quiet stretch the heave and slide.

Around us, spring's first flowers and
Fairer flowers women.

The timbre of Valery's French
(He's powder of bone beneath us)
Has spread through the mouth of our guide
Its self-calm more smooth over
Sea and air than cream
Sea-horses treading water
Before their vain dash up the rocks.

The foam proliferates, a short-lived,
Unsudden tropical tree;
Sea horses tread; spring flowers
And fairer women, and Valery are still;

In the plain beneath us
Against this moment's being
A grave-digger drums
Rhythm endless of endless life
Transmuted into stillness—
The central sea of being—

At mediterranean moments,

And so insistent after them.

Yet for you, too, Christ,
A grave-maker swung his spade

And then the resurrection.

GOODBYE (AFTER LORCA)

If I die
Leave the shutters open

The stumbling child reaches out startling
doves
Through open shutters I've seen him

The striding farmer presses plough to earth
Through open shutters I've seen him

If I die
Leave the shutters open

GOODBYE... DESPEDIDA

El niño come naranjas
Garcia Lorca

The boy leans on a coconut tree—
He's shaped like it without its leaves—
Tears the thick skin oily as the sea
And sucks the juicy flesh with carnal ease.

He does not know that leaves will fall
That long before a seed arranges
New roots he'll not hear us call,

Insensate as any sand to futile sound
He will not smell the sea, nor oranges
Lighting up his final ground.

John Figueroa was born in Jamaica in 1920. He has taught there and in the U.S.A., U.K. and Africa. He was the first native West Indian to be appointed to the post of professor at U.W.I. in 1957. He is currently an Honorary Fellow at the Centre for Caribbean Studies at the University of Warwick.

His publications include three previous books of poetry, *Blue Mountain Peaks* (1945), *Love Leaps Here* (1962) and *Ignoring Hurts* (1976); several anthologies of Caribbean writing including the *Anthology of African & Caribbean Writing in English* for the Open University; and a study of Education in the Caribbean: *Society, Schools and Progress in the West Indies* (1971). He was one of the authors of *Caribbean Writers: A Bio-Bibliographical-Critical Encyclopaedia* (1979). His poetry and criticism has appeared in countless journals, and his poetry has been recorded in the Caedmon Poets series.